Little People, BIG DREAMS™
BOB MARLEY

Written by
Maria Isabel Sánchez Vegara

Illustrated by
Subi Bosa

Frances Lincoln
Children's Books

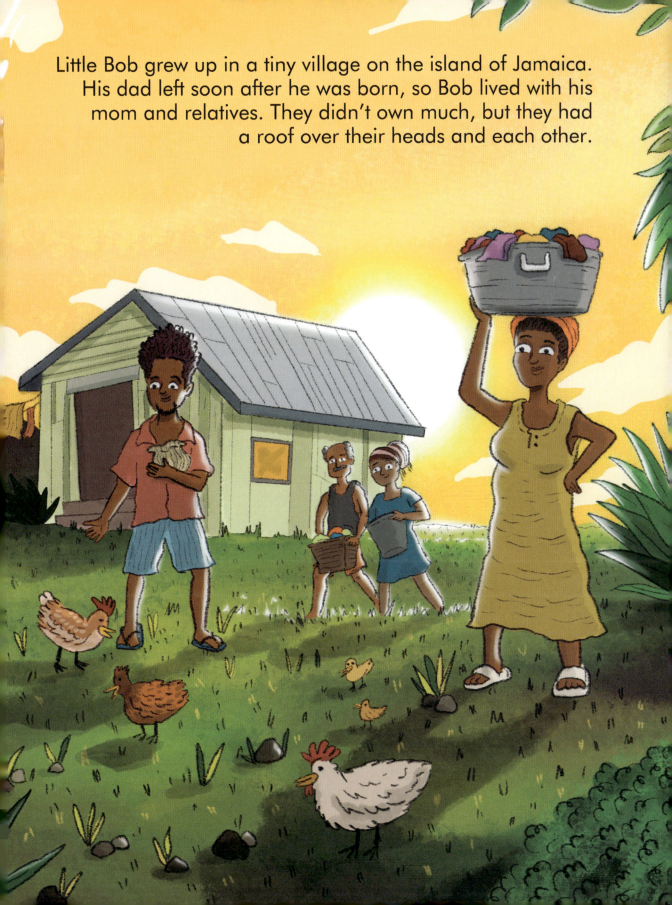

Little Bob grew up in a tiny village on the island of Jamaica. His dad left soon after he was born, so Bob lived with his mom and relatives. They didn't own much, but they had a roof over their heads and each other.

Growing up, life wasn't always easy for Bob. Some people picked on him because he was the child of a white man. Whenever that happened, Bob sought comfort in music, his one love.

Hoping for a better life, when Bob was twelve, he and his mom moved to Trench Town—a lively neighborhood in the city of Kingston. There, he discovered the coolest sound: ska. It blended new American music with old Caribbean beats.

Bob had left school and was working as an apprentice welder when he recorded his first song, "Judge Not." It wasn't a big hit, but it helped him get his old friend Bunny and a new friend, Peter, to join him in a band.

There was a lot to learn and many decisions to make. To overcome their fear of performing, Bob and his friends played in all sorts of places, even a graveyard!

They tried many names, but settled on The Wailers after their song "Simmer Down" topped the charts.

Everyone was dancing to their catchy music when Rita, Bob's girlfriend, introduced him to a Jamaican religion called Rastafari. It encouraged him to love nature, live peacefully, treat others with respect, and be proud of his African roots.

To spread the message and positive vibes of Rastafari, Bob and his friends started growing their hair into dreadlocks and moved on to a new relaxed sound called reggae. Soon, Bob's head was full of joyful jams and rebel anthems!

The Wailers were already big in Jamaica when they released *Catch a Fire* and *Burnin'*, and these albums helped spread their music abroad.

People loved their sound. It was as strong as rock, as groovy as pop, and as bold as punk . . . but with a reggae beat.

When Bunny and Peter left The Wailers, Rita and two other backup singers joined the band. With their help, the seed Bob had planted continued to grow, making him a symbol of Jamaican music and the biggest reggae star.

But while people around the world were singing his songs of peace and unity, his country was divided into two groups fighting for power. Back home, it felt like everyone had to be on one side or the other. Yet, Bob didn't want to choose.

. . . waking up early and only taking a break to play soccer.
This is how *Exodus*, his most celebrated album, was born.

The fighting in Jamaica was only getting worse, so Bob decided to go back and play in a peace concert. He brought the leaders of the two groups on stage, while people from both sides jammed together to his songs.

And by putting his heart and soul into his music, little Bob became a peacemaker, a kind rebel, and a legend: someone who made us all believe that every little thing is gonna be all right.

BOB MARLEY

(Born 1945 – Died 1981)

c. 1970

c. 1978

Bob Marley learned to play music while growing up in Nine Miles, a village in the Jamaican hills. When Bob was twelve, he and his mom moved to Trench Town, one of the poorest neighborhoods in Kingston, Jamaica's capital city. Life was tough, but Bob found joy in music, particularly ska—a new sound influenced by Caribbean folk music, jazz, and American R&B. In 1963, he formed a band with two friends, Neville "Bunny" Livingston and Peter Tosh, which they eventually called The Wailers. Their first single, "Simmer Down," gave a voice to the struggles of poor young Jamaicans, and topped the charts. In 1971, The Wailers got their big break when they were signed by the legendary Island Records label. Their next albums were worldwide hits, and Bob became a reggae superstar. His music was

1979   2024

passionate and political. In songs like "Get Up, Stand Up" and "One Love," he challenged injustice, urged people to fight for their rights, and called for peace, unity, and love. Meanwhile, Jamaica was becoming increasingly divided, and in 1976 Bob moved to London as a political refugee after he was injured in an attack in Kingston. Two years later, he returned to Jamaica to perform at the One Love Peace Concert. In a powerful moment of hope, he brought the leaders of the two fighting political parties onstage to join hands. Bob sadly died at the age of just thirty-six, but his legacy lives on. In 1999, his record *Exodus* was named Album of the Century, and in 2001, he was honored with the Grammy Lifetime Achievement Award. Today, Bob's music continues to unite and inspire people around the world.

Want to find out more?
Take a look at these great books:
Get Up, Stand Up by Bob Marley, Cedella Marley, and John Jay Cabuay
A History of Music for Children by Mary Richards, David Schweitzer, and Rose Blake

To my friend Emily, with endless wonder.

Text © 2025 Maria Isabel Sánchez Vegara. Illustrations © 2025 Subi Bosa
Original idea of the series by Maria Isabel Sánchez Vegara, published by Alba Editorial, s.l.u.
"Little People, BIG DREAMS" and "Pequeña & Grande" are trademarks of
Alba Editorial s.l.u. and/or Beautifool Couple S.L.
First Published in the U.S. in 2025 by Frances Lincoln Children's Books, an imprint of The Quarto Group.
100 Cummings Centre, Suite 265D, Beverly, MA 01915, USA. T +1 978-282-95900 www.Quarto.com
All rights reserved.
No part of this publication may be reproduced, stored in a retrieval system, or transmitted, in any form,
or by any means, electrical, mechanical, photocopying, recording, or otherwise without the prior written
permission of the publisher or a license permitting restricted copying.

This book is not authorized, licensed, or approved by the estate of Bob Marley.
Any faults are the publisher's who will be happy to rectify for future printings.
ISBN 978-1-83600-717-3
Set in Futura BT.

Published by Peter Marley · Edited by Molly Mead
Designed by Sasha Moxon, Izzy Bowman, and Karissa Santos
Production by Robin Boothroyd
Manufactured in Guangdong, China CC042025
1 3 5 7 9 8 6 4 2

Photographic acknowledgments (pages 28-29, from left to right): 1. Jamaican singer Bob Marley with The Wailers, circa 1970 © Michael Ochs Archives / Stringer via Getty Images. 2. Bob Marley Interview Vert. Portrait of Jamaican Reggae musician Bob Marley, circa 1978 © Allan Tannenbaum / Contributor / Archive Photos via Getty Images. 3. Jamaican reggae singer-songwriter Bob Marley (1945 – 1981), 27th November 1979 © Michael Ochs Archives / Stringer via Getty Images. 4. The Bob Marley Museum lights up in support of "Bob Marley: One Love" on January 22, 2024, in Kingston, Jamaica © Jason Koerner / Stringer / Getty Images South America via Getty Images.

Collect the Little People, BIG DREAMS™ series:

Scan the QR code for free activity sheets, teachers' notes and more information about the series at www.littlepeoplebigdreams.com